U.S.
ARMY

BY NICK GORDON

BELLWETHER MEDIA · MINNEAPOLIS, MN

EPIC BOOKS are no ordinary books. They burst with intense action, high-speed heroics, and shadows of the unknown. Are you ready for an Epic adventure?

This edition first published in 2013 by Bellwether Media, Inc.

No part of this publication may be reproduced in whole or in part without written permission of the publisher. For information regarding permission, write to Bellwether Media, Inc., Attention: Permissions Department, 5357 Penn Avenue South, Minneapolis, MN 55419.

Library of Congress Cataloging-in-Publication Data

Gordon, Nick.
 U.S. Army / by Nick Gordon.
     p. cm. – (Epic books: U.S. military)
 Includes bibliographical references and index.
 Summary: "Engaging images accompany information about the U.S. Army. The combination of high-interest subject matter and light text is intended for students in grades 2 through 7"–Provided by publisher.
 Audience: Grades 2-7.
 ISBN 978-1-60014-827-9 (hbk : alk. paper)
 1. United States. Army–Juvenile literature. I. Title.
 UA25.G63 2013
 355.00973–dc23
                              2012008555

Printed in the United States of America, North Mankato, MN.

TABLE OF CONTENTS

THE U.S. ARMY

The United States Army is a branch of the **United States Armed Forces**. Its main job is land warfare.

Army soldiers are grouped into **brigades**. Heavy brigades use tanks and other large vehicles. **Infantry** brigades are for light combat. Army members who fly or repair aircraft serve in airborne brigades.

UNITED STATES ARMY

Founded: 1775

Headquarters: Arlington, Virginia

Motto: "This We'll Defend"

Size: More than 500,000 active personnel

Major Engagements: Revolutionary War, War of 1812, American Civil War, World War I, World War II, Korean War, Vietnam War, Gulf War, Kosovo War, Iraq War, Afghanistan War, War on Terror

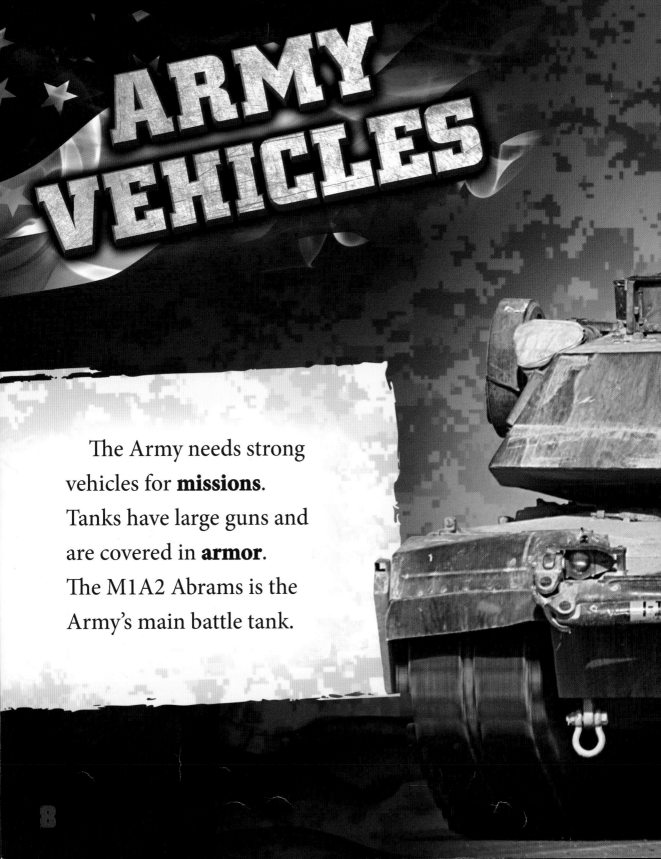

ARMY VEHICLES

The Army needs strong vehicles for **missions**. Tanks have large guns and are covered in **armor**. The M1A2 Abrams is the Army's main battle tank.

M1A2 ABRAMS

Armored troop carriers transport soldiers. The Stryker can carry up to nine soldiers and their gear.

ARMY FACT

The Stryker is named after two soldiers who won the Medal of Honor. This award is the Army's highest honor.

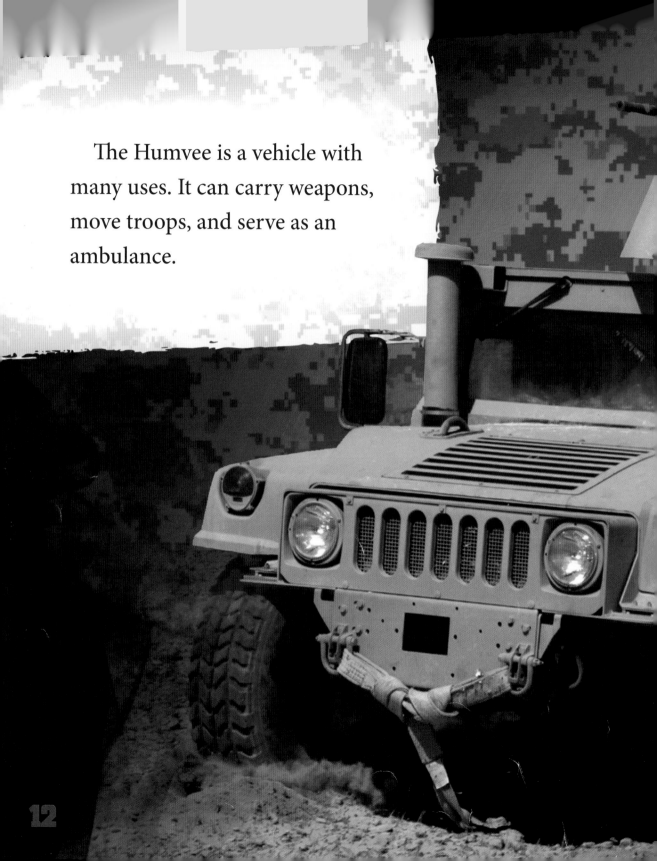

The Humvee is a vehicle with many uses. It can carry weapons, move troops, and serve as an ambulance.

HUMVEE

The Army also uses aircraft. The AH-64 Apache is an attack helicopter. It is loaded with **missiles** and other weapons. The UH-60 Black Hawk transports troops.

UH-60 BLACK HAWK

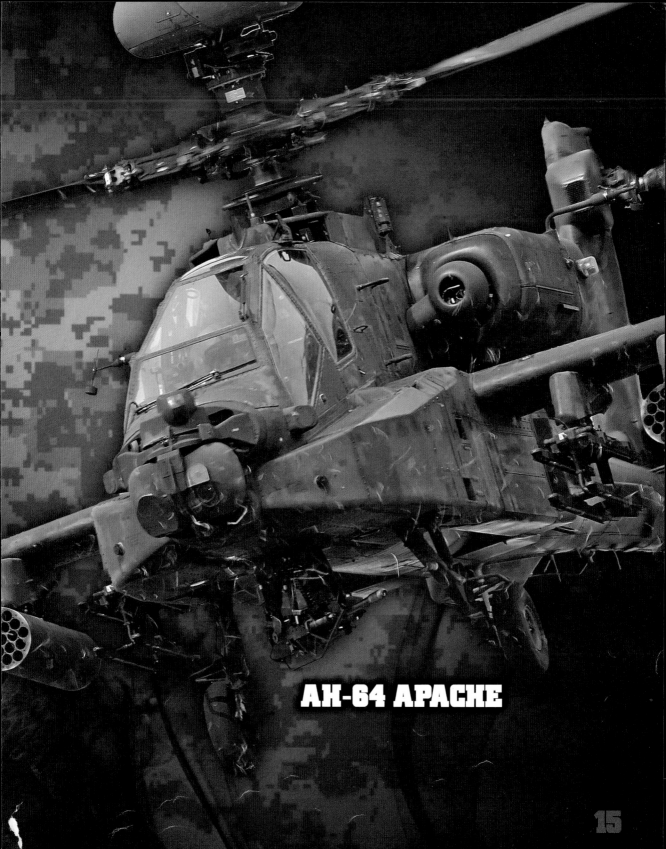

AH-64 APACHE

ARMY MISSIONS

The Army's main mission is defense. Soldiers fight on land to defend the U.S. and its **allies**.

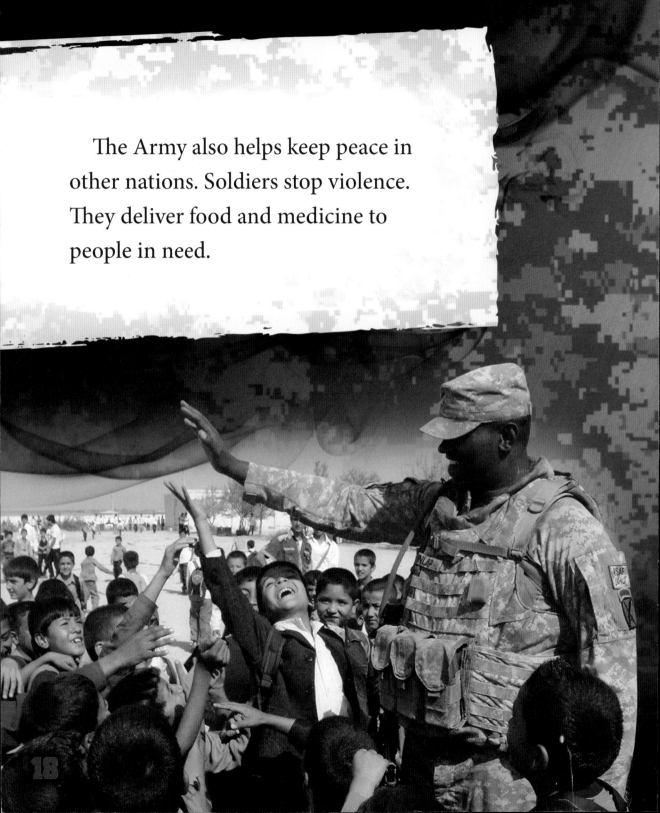

The Army also helps keep peace in other nations. Soldiers stop violence. They deliver food and medicine to people in need.

ARMY FACT

Around 200,000 soldiers serve in the Army Reserve. They train every month in case they are called to active duty.

The U.S. Army is the most powerful army in the world. Its vehicles and weapons make it strong. Its brave men and women make it stronger!

GLOSSARY

allies—friendly nations that have common goals or purposes; the United States has many allies around the world.

armor—thick plates that cover a vehicle to protect its crew

brigades—divisions of the U.S. Army; a brigade includes soldiers who perform a common mission.

infantry—ground troops

missiles—explosives that are guided to a target

missions—military tasks

United States Armed Forces—the five branches of the United States military; they are the Air Force, the Army, the Coast Guard, the Marine Corps, and the Navy.

TO LEARN MORE

At the Library

David, Jack. *United States Army*. Minneapolis, Minn.: Bellwether Media, 2008.

Gordon, Nick. *Army Rangers*. Minneapolis, Minn.: Bellwether Media, 2013.

Hamilton, John. *The Army*. Edina, Minn.: ABDO Pub., 2007.

On the Web

Learning more about the U.S. Army is as easy as 1, 2, 3.

1. Go to www.factsurfer.com.

2. Enter "U.S. Army" into the search box.

3. Click the "Surf" button and you will see a list of related Web sites.

With factsurfer.com, finding more information is just a click away.

INDEX